Canadian Citizenship Workbook

Drew Smith

BeaverMaple.ca

The *Canadian Citizenship Workbook* is to be used alongside the official government guide *Discover Canada*. You can download a free copy of *Discover Canada* on www.canada.ca.

Memorization is an important part of passing the Canadian Citizenship Exam. Working through the following exercises will help you retain all of the pertinent information needed to successfully pass the Canadian Citizenship Exam.

Index

1.Being Canadian

Complete the sentence by matching two fragments.

1)Queen Elizabeth II

a) outlines the freedoms and rights that Canadians enjoy.

2)The Magna Carta

b) is not compulsory in Canada.

3)The Canadian Forces

c) have equal status under the law.

4)In 1982

d) is a responsibility that Canadians should uphold.

5)The Charter of Rights and Freedoms

e) allow Canadians to work and live anywhere in Canada.

6)Men and women

f) helped to amend the Constitution in 1982.

7)Voting in elections

g) have equal status in Parliament.

8)Mobility Rights

h) was signed in 1215 in England.

9)French and English

i) the Constitution was amended.

10)Military service

j) defend Canada.

2. Right, Responsibility or Freedom

Write *freedom*, *responsibility* or *right* under the following:

1.Canadians can work and live anywhere in Canada.

_____

2.Canadians should vote in elections.

_____

3.French and English have equal status in Parliament and the government.

_____

4.Canadians can peacefully assemble.

_____

5.Canadians can practice any religion.

_____

6.Canadians are expected to help in their community.

_____

7.Canadians are allowed to speak freely.

_____

8.Canadians must try to work and take care of the family.

_____

3. Rights and Responsibilities – Part 1

1.List three sources of Canadian law:

-
-
-

2.What is Habeas Corpus?

_____

3.What was added to the Canadian Constitution in 1982?

_____

4.How can Canadians help defend their community and country? List three ways.

-
-
-

4. Rights and Responsibilities – Part 2

1. Write four freedoms that Canadians enjoy:

   -

   -

   -

   -

2. Write three rights that Canadians enjoy:

   -

   -

   -

3. Write three responsibilities that Canadians must uphold:

   -

   -

   -

5. The People of Canada – Questions

1.Who are the three founding peoples of Canada?

-
-
-

2.Who are the three aboriginal peoples of Canada?

-
-
-

3.Who are the First Nations?

_____

4.Who are the Inuit?

_____

5.Who are the Métis?

_____

6. First Nations, Inuit or Métis

Write First Nations, Inuit or Métis beside the following statements.

1._____ - speak the Inuktitut language.

2._____ - half of this group lives on reserve land.

3._____- have a mixed Aboriginal and European ancestry.

4._____ -make up 65% of Aboriginal Peoples in Canada.

5._____ - mostly live in the Arctic.

6._____- make up 30% of Aboriginals Peoples in Canada.

7._____- speak the dialect Michif.

8._____- make up 4% of Aboriginal Peoples in Canada.

7. The People of Canada – Part 1

Place the following vocabulary in the sentences below.

Anglophones	Acadians	Quebecers	The Great Upheaval
Francophones	Bilingual	New Brunswick	English, Welsh, Scottish and Irish

1. _____ speak French as a first language.

2. The _____ are the people of Quebec.

3. _____ is the only official bilingual province.

4. The _____ are descended from French colonists.

5. Many Anglophones in Canada are descended from the _____ immigrants who came to Canada from the seventeenth century onwards.

6. _____ people can speak two languages.

7. _____ speak English as a first language.

8. During _____ many Acadians were deported from their native land.

8. The People of Canada – Part 2

Place one of the following numbers in the statements below.

1604	2006	one million
eighteen million	1755 and 1763	seven million

1. There are _____ Francophones living in Ontario.

2. In _____ the House of Commons declared that the Quebecois form a nation within a united Canada.

3. There are _____ Francophones in Canada.

4. French colonist began settling along the east coast of what is now Canada in _____.

5. The Great Upheaval took place between _____.

6. There are over _____ Anglophones in Canada.

9. The People of Canada – Part 3

Correct the mistake in each sentence.

1.There are three aboriginal groups in Canada: First Nations, Inuit and Acadian.

2. The Quebecois were deported from their homeland during the Great Upheaval.

3.The three founding peoples of Canada are: the Aboriginal, the British and the United Empire Loyalists.

4.A Francophone speaks English as their first language.

5.The name Inuit means "the settlers" in Inuktitut.

6.The Acadians are descendants of Welsh colonists who settled along the east coast.

7.Quebec is the only officially bilingual province in Canada.

8.The Métis speak the language Inuktitut.

9.The Quebecers only speak French.

10.There are no Francophones living in Ontario.

10. The Diversity of Canada

Answer the following questions.

1. Who was a famous Governor General that stated, "Immigrant groups should retain their individuality and each make its contribution to the national character?"

_____

2. What is the largest religious affiliation in Canada?

_____

3. Besides English and French, what languages are spoken the most in Canadian homes?

_____

4. From which important document is the phrase, "Peace, Order and Good Government?"

_____

5. Who are the three founding peoples of Canada?

_____

6. Who are the three Aboriginal groups of Canada?

_____

11. Early Explorers

Write either John Cabot, Jacques Cartier or Samuel de Champlain in the spaces below.

1. _____ claimed the newly found land for King Francis I of France.

2. _____ was the first to draw a map of the Atlantic shore of what is now Canada.

3. _____ built a fortress at present-day Quebec city.

4._____ heard two guides say the Iroquoian word *kanata*.

5._____ first set foot on Newfoundland (or Cape Breton island) in 1497.

6. _____ built alliances with various Aboriginal groups.

12. Early Canadian History

Answer the following questions.

1. Which group from Iceland first reached Newfoundland and Labrador over 1000 years ago?

_____

2. What is the name of the World Heritage Site that houses the remains of their settlement?

_____

3. What two groups made peace in 1701?

_____

4. What animal drove the fur trade economy?

_____

5. Which company was granted the trading rights to the Hudson Bay watershed?

_____

6. Who were the *voyageurs* and *coureur de bois*?

_____

7. What famous battle occurred in 1759 between France and Great Britain?

_____

8. What was the outcome of the Battle of the Plains of Abraham?

_____

13. The Battle of the Plains of Abraham

Read the statement and circle T(true) or F(false).

1.The Battle of the Plains of Abraham took place in the year 1759. T/F

2.The Battle of the Plains of Abraham took place in Montreal. T/F

3.The British and the French battled for control of North America. T/F

4.The battle marked the end of the French Empire in North America. T/F

5. Brigadier James Wolfe was the commander for the British army. T/F

6.Samuel de Champlain was the commander of the French army. T/F/

7.The French defeated the British at the Battle of the Plains of Abraham. T/F

8.Both the British and French commanders died in the Battle. T/F

14. After the Battle of the Plains of Abraham

Fill in the blanks with the vocabulary below.

Quebec Act	habitants	freedom	Roman Catholic
Province of Quebec	Canadiens	1774	

1.After the Battle of the Plains of Abraham, the French colony was renamed the _____.

2.The French were also known as _____ and _____.

3.The majority of the French followed the _____ religion.

4.The Quebec Act was passed in _____.

5.The Quebec Act allowed the French religious _____.

6.The _____ also allowed the French to hold public office.

15. United Empire Loyalists

Answer the following questions.

1.In which year did the thirteen British colonies of what is now the United States of America declare independence?

_____

2.How many loyalists fled the revolution and settled in Nova Scotia and Quebec?

_____

3.To whom were the United Empire Loyalists loyal?

_____

4.Which famous Mohawk leader led thousands of loyalist Mohawk Indians to what is now Canada?

_____

5.From what ethnic backgrounds did the loyalists come?

_____

6.From which religious background did the loyalists come?

_____

7.About how many black Loyalists, freedmen and slaves fled to what is now Canada?

_____

16. Slavery in British North America

Answer the questions below.

1.Who helped Upper Canada become the first province in the British Empire to abolish slavery?

_____

2.Who was Upper Canada's first Lieutenant Governor?

_____

3.Lieutenant John Graves Simcoe was the founder of the City of York. What is this city called today?

_____

4.In which year was slavery abolished throughout the British Empire?

_____

5.Who became the first female publisher in Canada in 1853?

_____

6.What was the *Provincial Freeman* newspaper about?

_____

7.Who followed the North Star to Canada?

_____

8.What was the Underground Railway?

_____

17. The War of 1812 – Part 1

Write a famous person in each of the spaces below.

1. He was the leader of the Shawnee who supported the British in the War of 1812.

_____

2. This British Major-General was killed at Queenston Heights.

_____

3. He, alongside 460 soldiers defeated the American invaders at Chateauguay in 1813.

_____

4. He led an invasion that burned down the White House and other buildings in Washington, D.C.

_____

5. She warned the British of a probable American attack by travelling 30km on foot.

_____

6. He was warned by Laura Secord of a planned American attack.

_____

18. The War of 1812 – Part 2

Circle either T(true) or F(false). Correct the statement if it is false.

1. Canada launched an invasion of the United States of America in 1812. T/F

2. British soldiers, Canadian volunteers and First Nations all worked together to defend Canada. T/F

3. Sir Isaac Brock was killed at the Battle of Beaver Dams. T/F

4. Chief Tecumseh was a British leader. T/F

5. In 1813, Americans burned down parts of York (Toronto). T/F

6. Laura Secord warned the British of an American attack by canoeing for 30 km. T/F

7. The British lost the Battle of Beaver Dams. T/F

8. By 1814 the Americans had lost the war. T/F

19. Before Confederation

Answer the question below.

1.Where did the Rebellions of 1837-1838 take place?

_____

2.Who was sent by Britain to report on the rebellions?

_____

3.What did Lord Durham recommend?

_____

4.In which year was the Province of Canada formed?

_____

5.In which year did Nova Scotia become the first British North American colony to gain a full responsible government?

_____

6.Who became the first head of a responsible government in 1849?

_____

7.Who suggested the term *Dominion of Canada* in 1864?

_____

20. Confederation – Part 1

Use the vocabulary to complete the sentences below.

Sir John A. Macdonald	Sir George-Ettiene Cartier	1867	The Dominion of Canada
Ontario	Dominion Day	Canada Day	legislature

1. The British North America Act was passed in _____ by the British Parliament.

2. The first four provinces of Canada were _____, Quebec, Nova Scotia and New Brunswick.

3. _____, a lawyer from Quebec was a major architect of Confederation.

4. _____ is celebrated on July, 1st.

5. In 1867, _____ officially became a country.

6. _____ became the first Prime Minister of Canada in 1867.

7. Before 1982, Canada Day was known as _____.

8. After Confederation, each province would have its own _____.

21. Confederation – Part 2

Answer the following questions below.

1.In which year was the British North America Act passed?

_____

2.On which date was the Dominion of Canada officially created?

_____

3.What were the first four provinces of the Dominion of Canada?

_____

4.What was the last province to join Canada in 1949?

_____

5.What was the last territory to join Canada in 1999?

_____

6.What was Canada Day called before 1982?

_____

7.Who became the first Prime Minister of Canada in 1867?

_____

8.From which country did Sir John A. Macdonald emigrate as a child?

_____

9.On which Canadian banknote is Sir John A. Macdonald?

_____

10.On which date is Sir John A. Macdonald Day celebrated?

_____

22. Confederation – Part 3

Fill in the missing information from the chart. Write either a province/territory, or the year in which the province/territory joined Canada.

Province	Year
1. Ontario	
2. Prince Edward Island	
3.	1871
4.	1867
5. Alberta	
6. Quebec	
7.	1870
8.	1905
9. Newfoundland and Labrador	
10. New Brunswick	

Territory	Year
1. Norwest Territories	
2. Yukon	
3.	1999

23. Louis Riel

Answer the following questions.

1.What did Louis Riel and his supporters take control of in 1869?

_____

2.Of which aboriginal group was Louis Riel a leader?

_____

3.Where did Louis Riel flee to after the government sent military support?

_____

4.What was the outcome for Louis Riel after a second Rebellion in 1885?

_____

5.Who was the Métis' greatest military leader?

_____

6.Which police force did Sir John A. Macdonald create after the Métis rebellions?

_____

7.Who was Sir Sam Steele?

_____

8.What is the name of Canada's federal police force today?

_____

24. The Canadian Pacific Railway

Place the following words in the sentences below.

Sir Wilfrid Laurier	Head Tax	unity	Ukranians
Lord Strathcona	British Columbia	1885	railway

1. The Canadian Pacific Railway was completed in _____.

2. _____ drove in the last railway spike.

3. The Canadian Pacific Railway symbolized _____.

4. The _____ was built by Chinese and European workers.

5. _____ joined the Dominion of Canada in 1871 due to the fact that Ottawa promised to complete a railway.

6. The first French-Canadian Prime Minster was _____.

7. After the railway was completed, thousands of immigrants, including 170,000 _____ settled in the West.

8. After the railway was completed, Chinese immigrants were forced to pay a discriminatory _____ upon entering Canada.

25. Women of Canada – Part 1

Answer the following questions.

1.Which province first granted voting rights to women in 1916?

_____

2.What does the word *suffrage* mean?

_____

3.Who was the founder of the women's suffrage movement in Canada?

_____

4.Which Prime Minister first gave women the right to vote in federal elections?

_____

5.In which year were most women over the age of 21 granted the right to vote in federal elections?

_____

6.Who became the first female MP in 1921?

_____

7.In which year did Quebec grant women the right to vote?

_____

8.Who were the *bluebirds*?

_____

26. Women of Canada – Part 2

Write the name of an important Canadian woman/women beside the following statements.

1._____ - became the first female MP in 1921.

2._____ - an important politician and feminist from Quebec.

3._____ - the first Canadian woman to practice medicine in Canada.

4._____ - the nickname of the nurses who served in the Royal Canadian Army Canadian Corps.

5._____ - the founder of the women's suffrage movement in Canada.

27. The First World War – Part 1

Answer the following questions.

1.In which year did the First World War begin?

_____

2.On which date did the First World War end?

_____

3.How many Canadians served in the First World War?

_____

4.How many Canadians were killed in the First World War?

_____

5.Who was regarded as Canada's greatest solider?

_____

6.What did the Canadian army capture in April 1917?

_____

7.Which important battle that took place on August 8, 1918, did the Germans call "the black day of the German Army?"

_____

28. The First World War – Part 2

Put a number in the spaces provided.

1914	600,000	10,000	9
1918	60,000	8,000	11

1. Over _____ Canadians served in the First World War.

2. At the Battle of Vimy Ridge, _____ soldiers were killed or injured.

3. The war ended on November _____, _____.

4. In the end, _____ Canadians were killed in battle.

5. Unforuntately, over _____ Austro-Hungarians immigrants were put in labour camps across Canada.

6. The First World War began in _____.

7. Vimy Day is recognized every year on April _____.

29. Remembrance Day

Answer the following questions

1.When is Remembrance Day observed in Canada?

_____

2.Who wrote the poem *In Flanders Fields*?

_____

3.Who was John McCrae?

_____

4.What do Canadians wear on Remembrance Day?

_____

5.What do Canadians do at 11:00 am on Remembrance Day?

_____

6.In which year was *In Flanders Fields* composed?

_____

7.What are the first two lines of *In Flanders Fields*?

_____

_____

30. The Second World War

Answer the following questions.

1. In which year did the Second World War begin?

_____

2. How many Canadians (and Newfoundlanders) served in the Second World War?

_____

3. Which part of the Canadian Forces played an important role in the Battle of Britain and in other battles across Europe?

_____

4. What did the Canadian Government apologize for in 1988?

_____

5. What is June 6th, 1944 also known as?

_____

6. How many Canadian soldiers attacked Juno Beach on D-Day?

_____

7. On which date did Germany surrender?

_____

8. How many Canadians were killed in the Second World War?

_____

31. Post-War Canada

Circle either T (true) or F (false). Correct the statement if it is false.

1. Oil was discovered in Manitoba in 1947. T/F

2. Unemployment insurance was introduced in 1950. T/F

3. Five hundred Canadians died during the Korean War (1950-53). T/F

4. The Official Languages Act of 1969 gave both English and French equal status in the government of Canada. T/F

5. The Canadian Constitution was amended in 1982. T/F

6. In 1980 Canada helped found La Francophonie. T/F

7. Japanese Canadians received the right to vote in 1938. T/F

8. Aborginal people received the right to vote in 1960. T/F

32. Arts in Canada

Write the following names under the headings below.

Denys Arcand	Rohinton Mistry	Ernest Macmillan	Emily Carr
Kenojuak Ashevak	Atom Egoyan	Michael Odaatje	Healey Willan

Writers:

-
-

Visual Artists:

-
-

Filmmakers:

-
-

Musicians:

-
-

33. Sports in Canada

Answer the following questions.

1. Who invented basketball in 1891?

_____

2. What is Canada's official summer sport?

_____

3. What is Canada's official winter sport?

_____

4. Who started the Marathon of Hope in 1980?

_____

5. What Edmonton Oiler was perhaps the greatest hockey player of all time?

_____

6. Who travelled around in the world in a wheelchair in 1985?

_____

7. Who is a famous Canadian sprinter that has two Olympic gold medals?

_____

8. Who scored the game-winning goal for Canada in the 1971 Canada-Soviet hockey game?

_____

34. Inventions and Discoveries – Part 1

Match the person with their invention or discovery.

1.Sir Frederick Banting	a)telephone
2.Reginald Fessenden	b)snowmobile
3.Alexander Graham Bell	c)pacemaker
4.Sir Sanford Fleming	d)electric lightbulb
5.Joseph-Armand Bombardier	e)insulin
6.Dr.John A. Hopps	f)blackberry
7.Matthew Evans	g)radio
8.Mike Lazaridis	h)standard time zones

35. Inventions and Discoveries – Part 2

Answer the following questions.

1.Who discovered insulin?

_____

2.Who invented the first cardiac pacemaker?

_____

3.Who invented the first electric light bulb?

_____

4.Who invented the telephone?

_____

5.Who invented the system of standard time zones?

_____

6.Who sent the first wireless voice message?

_____

7.Who are the founders of Research in Motion?

_____

8.Who invented the snowmobile?

_____

36. Canadian Government – Part 1

Answer the following questions.

1. What are three important facts about Canada's system of government?

-

-

-

2. What are the three parts of Parliament?

-

-

-

3. What are the three branches of the Canadian Government?

-

-

-

37. Canadian Government – Part 2

Answer the following questions.

1. What are three responsibilities of the federal government?

_____

2. In which part of Parliament do the elected Members of Parliament work?

_____

3. Who selects the Cabinet ministers?

_____

4. Who works in the Senate?

_____

5. The House of Commons and the Senate discuss and review bills. What is a *bill*?

_____

6. What is the final step in which a bill becomes an official law?

_____

7. Who is Canada's Head of State?

_____

8. Who is Canada's Head of Government?

_____

38. Canadian Government – Part 3

Place the name of a person in the spaces below.

Prime Minister	Sovereign	Lieutenant Governor	Governor General
Member of Parliament	Senator	Premier	Commissioner

1._____ - represents the Sovereign in the federal government.

2._____ - works in the Senate.

3._____ - is Canada's head of government.

4._____ - works in the House of Commons.

5._____ - represents the Sovereign in the provincial government.

6._____ - is the head of a provincial government.

7._____ - is Canada's head of state.

8._____ - represents the federal government in a territory.

39. Federal Elections – Part 1

Answer the following questions.

1.On which day are federal elections held in Canada?

_____

2.How many electoral districts are there in Canada?

_____

3.Who do people vote for in federal elections?

_____

4.Who can vote in elections? List three criteria.

-

-

-

5.What is a government called if it has at least half of the seats in the House of Commons?

_____

6.What is a government called if it has less than half of the seats in the House of Commons?

_____

40. Federal Elections – Part 2

Answer the following questions.

1.Who chooses the Cabinet ministers?

_____

2.What is the responsibility of a cabinet minister?

_____

3.What is the political party that has the second most members in the House of Commons called?

_____

4.Which political party is currently in power?

_____

5.What political party is currently the Official Opposition?

_____

6.What are the names of other political parties that are currently represented in the House of Commons?

_____

41. Federal Government – Questions

Complete the following information.

1.Who is the Prime Minister of Canada?

_____

2.To which political party does the Prime Minister belong?

_____

3.How many seats in the House of Commons does the party in power have?

_____

4.Who is your Member of Parliament?

_____

5.To which political party does your MP belong?

_____

6.Which political party is the Official Opposition?

_____

7.How many seats does the Official Opposition have?

_____

8.Who is the leader of the Official Opposition party?

_____

42. Municipal Government

Answer the following questions.

1.Who is the head of a municipal government?

_____

2.Who is the mayor of your city?

_____

3.Who is your councillor?

_____

4.What type of laws can municipal governments pass?

_____

5.What are three responsibilities of a municipal government?

-
-
-

43. Provincial Government

Answer the following questions.

1.Who is the premier of your province?

_____

2.To which political party does your premier belong?

_____

3.Who is your MPP (or MLA, MNA, or MHA)?

_____

4.To which political party do they belong?

_____

5.What are three responsibilities of a provincial government?

-
-
-

6.Who is the lieutenant governor of your province?

_____

7.In which city is your legislative assembly?

_____

44. Justice in Canada

Circle either T (true) or F (false). Correct the statement if it is false.

1.In Canada, you are guilty until proven innocent. T/F

2.In Canada, the law applies to everyone. T/F

3.The Supreme Court of Canada is Canada's highest court. T/F

4.The RCMP is Canada's federal police force. T/F

5.Ontario and Manitoba have their own provincial police force. T/F

6.The RCMP serves as the provincial police force in all provinces. T/F

45. The Symbols of Canada – Part 1

Complete the sentence by matching the two columns.

1. The Canadian Flag

2. The Beaver

3. The Maple Leaf

4. The Fleur-de-Lys

5. A mari usque ad mare

6. Hockey

7. Lacrosse

8. The Parliament Buildings

a) is on the Canadian flag.

b) are located in Ottawa.

c) is on the Canadian nickel.

d) means from sea to sea in Latin.

e) is Canada's official winter sport.

f) was first used in 1965.

g) is on the flag of Quebec.

h) is Canada's official summer sport.

46. The Symbols of Canada – Part 2

Answer the following questions.

1. For how long has the Canadian Crown been a symbol of Canada?

_____

2. In which year was the red and white Canadian Flag first raised?

_____

3. What is Canada's official summer sport?

_____

4. What happened to part of the Parliament buildings in 1916?

_____

5. In which year was the Peace Tower completed?

_____

6. What is Canada's motto? What does it mean in English?

_____

7. In which year did Quebec adopt its own flag?

_____

8. What symbol is carved into the headstones of Canadian soldiers?

_____

47.The Crown in Canada

Answer the following questions.

1.What is the national anthem of Canada?

_____

2.What is the royal anthem of Canada?

_____

3.What is the royal flag of Canada called?

_____

4.In which year was the red and white Canadian flag first raised?

_____

5.Who was the Queen of England in 1867?

_____

6.Who represents the Sovereign in the federal government?

_____

7.Besides Canada, what are three other countries that are part of the British Commonwealth of Nations?

_____

8.Who is the current Head of State in Canada?

_____

48. The Victoria Cross

Answer the following questions.

1. How many Canadians have received the Victoria Cross?

_____

2. Who was the first Canadian to be awarded the Victoria Cross?

_____

3. Which famous *flying ace* won a Victoria Cross for his service in the First World War?

_____

4. Who was the first black man to be awarded the Victoria Cross?

_____

5. Who was the last recipient of the Victoria Cross?

_____

6. Who was awarded the Victoria Cross for his bravery in the Battle of Hill 70 in 1917?

_____

7. In which war did Victoria Cross recipient Captain Paul Triquet serve?

_____

49. The Canadian Economy

Answer the following questions.

1.Which three countries are part of NAFTA?

_____

2.In which year did free trade with the United States of America begin?

_____

3.What are Canada's three main types of industries?

-
-
-

4.In which industry are most Canadians employed?

_____

5.Which industry includes fishing, mining and agriculture?

_____

6.Which industry includes aerospace technology, food and automobiles?

_____

7.Which country is Canada's largest trading partner?

_____

8.What percentage of Canadian exports head to the United States of America?

_____

50. Canadian Geography – Overview

Answer the following questions.

1. What three oceans surround Canada?

_____

2. What is the capital of Canada?

_____

3. In which year was the capital of Canada chosen?

_____

4. How many provinces and territories does Canada have?

_____

5. What is the population of Canada?

_____

6. How many regions does Canada have?

_____

7. What are the five regions of Canada?

-
-
-
-
-

51. The Regions of Canada – Part 1

Place the names of the provinces and territories under the correct region.

1. The Atlantic Provinces

-
-
-
-

2. Central Canada

-
-

3. The Prairie Provinces

-
-
-

4. The West Coast

-

5. The Northern Territories

-
-
-

52. The Regions of Canada – Part 2

Answer the following questions.

1. Which region borders the Arctic Ocean?

_____

2. Which region contains more than half of the population in Canada?

_____

3. Which region is on the East Coast of Canada?

_____

4. Which region is well known for its fertile farmland?

_____

5. Which region contains the busiest Canadian port?

_____

6. Which large region has a population of only one hundred thousand?

_____

7. Which region manufactures more than three-quarters of all Canadian goods?

_____

8. In which region can daylight last up to 24 hours in the summer?

_____

53. The Regions of Canada – Part 3

Fill in the missing information in the chart below.

Region	Provinces or Territories
• The West Coast	•
•	• Alberta • •
• Central Canada	• •
•	• Prince Edward Island • • • Newfoundland and Labrador
• The Northern Territories	• • •

54. The Canadian Provinces

Write the name of the province or territory that is associated with the statement.

1._____ - the largest producer of hydro-electricity

2._____ - has the world's highest tides at the Bay of Fundy

3._____ - it has its own time zone

4._____ - the only official bilingual province

5._____ - it has the most valuable forestry industry in Canada

6._____ - is known for potatoes and Anne of Green Gables

7._____ - it was established in 1999

8._____ - the largest producer of oil and gas

9._____ - has Western Canada's largest francophone community

10._____ - has the record for the coldest recorded temperature in Canada

11._____ - is home to the Great Lakes

12._____ - is home to the training centre of the RCMP

13._____ - its capital is known as *the diamond capital of North America*

55. Provincial and Territorial Capitals

Complete the following chart.

Province	Capital
British Columbia	
	Regina
	Fredericton
Alberta	
Prince Edward Island	
	Quebec City
Ontario	
Manitoba	
	Halifax
	St.John's

Territory	Capital
Yukon	
	Iqaluit
Northwest Territories	

56. Capital Cities

Write the Province or Territory beside its capital city.

1. Victoria - _____

2. Fredericton - _____

3. Regina - _____

4. Halifax - _____

5. Toronto - _____

6. Iqaluit - _____

7. Charlottetown - _____

8. Whitehorse - _____

9. St. John's - _____

10. Edmonton - _____

11. Quebec City - _____

12. Yellowknife - _____

13. Winnipeg - _____

57. Canadian Provinces and Territories

Correct the mistake (highlighted in *italics*) in the sentences below.

1. *Quebec* is the only officially bilingual province.

2. The capital of British Columbia is *Vancouver*.

3. The Mackenzie River is located in *Quebec*.

4. *Saskatchewan* is home to Banff National Park.

5. *Fredericton* is the largest port on the east coast of Canada.

6. *Vancouver* is Canada's second largest city.

7. *New Brunswick* is known for the fruit and wine industries of the Okanagan Valley.

8. *Nova Scotia* is the birthplace of Confederation.

58. Review Questions – Part 1

Answer the following questions.

1. What are three important aspects about Canada's system of government?

-
-
-

2. What are the three levels of government in Canada?

-
-
-

3. What are the three branches of government in Canada?

-
-
-

4. What are the three parts of Parliament?

-
-
-

59. Review Questions – Part 2

Answer the following questions.

1. Who are the three founding peoples of Canada?

-
-
-

2. What are the three distinct Aboriginal peoples of Canada?

-
-
-

3. Who is Canada's head of government?

_____

4. Who is Canada's head of state?

_____

5. What is the only officially bilingual province in Canada?

_____

60. Review Questions – Political Review

1. Who is the current Prime Minister of Canada?

_____

2. Who is your Member of Parliament?

_____

3. Who is the Governor General of Canada?

_____

4. Who is the Premier of your province?

_____

5. Who is your MPP (MLA, MNA, or MHA)?

_____

6. Who is the Lieutenant Governor of your province?

_____

7. Who is the mayor of your city?

_____

8. Who is your city councillor?

_____

Answer Key

1.Being a Canadian

1. - f)
2. - h)
3. - j)
4. - i)
5. - a)
6. - c)
7. - d)
8. - e)
9. - g)
10. -b)

2.Right, Responsibility or Freedom

1.right
2.responsibility
3.right
4.freedom
5.freedom
6.responsibility
7.freedom
8.responsibility

3.Rights and Responsibilities – Part 1

1. List three sources of Canadian law:
   - Parliament and Provincial Legislatures
   - English Common Law
   - Civil Code of France

2. Habeas Corpus is the right to challenge a detention by the country. (i.e. someone can not be held in detention unless it is first decided by a court that it is legal to do so)

3. The Canadian Charter of Rights and Freedoms

4. How can Canadians help defend their community and country? List three ways.

- Serve in the Canadian Forces
- Serve in your local militia/navy or reserves
- You can serve in the Coast Guard or other emergency services such as the fire department or police force.

4.Rights and Responsibilities – Part 2

1. Write four freedoms that Canadians enjoy:
- Freedom of conscience and religion
- Freedom of thought, belief, opinion and expression, freedom of speech and freedom of the press
- Freedom to peaceful assembly
- Freedom of association

2. Write three rights that Canadians enjoy:
- Official Language Rights
- Mobility Rights
- Aboriginal Peoples' Rights

3. Write three responsibilities that Canadians must uphold:
- Obeying the law
- Serving on a jury
- Voting in elections

5.The People of Canada – Questions

1.Aboriginal, British and French
2.First Nations, Métis and Inuit
3.The Aboriginal Peoples that are not Inuit or Métis are First Nations. Before 1970, the term Indian was used.
4.The Inuit are an aboriginal group that mainly live in the arctic and speak Inuktitut.
5.The Métis are an aboriginal group of mixed Aboriginal and European ancestry.

6.First Nations, Inuit or Métis

1.Inuit

2. First Nations

3. Métis

4. First Nations

5. Inuit

6. Métis

7. Métis.

8. Inuit

7.The People of Canada – Part 1

1.Francophone
2.Quebecers
3. New Brunswick
4. Acadians
5. English, Welsh, Scottish and Irish
6. Bilingual
7. Anglophone
8. The Great Upheaval

8.The People of Canada – Part 2

1. One million
2. 2006
3. Seven million
4.1604
5.1755 and 1763
6.Eighteen million

9.The People of Canada – Part 3

1.There are three aboriginal groups in Canada: First Nations, Inuit and **Métis**.

2. The **Acadians** were deported from their homeland during the Great Upheaval.

3.The three founding peoples of Canada are: the Aboriginal, the British and the **French**.

4. A Francophone speaks **French** as their first language.

5.The name Inuit means "**the people**" in Inuktitut.

6. The Acadians are descendants of **French** colonists who settled along the east coast.

7.**New Brunswick** is the only officially bilingual province in Canada.

8.The **Inuit** speak the language Inuktitut.

9.The Quebecers speak **French and English**. (The majority are French-speaking).

10.There are **one million** Francophones living in Ontario.

10.The Diversity of Canada

1.John Buchan
2.Catholic
3.Chinese languages
4.The British North America Act of 1867
5.Aborginal, French and British
6.First Nations, Métis and Inuit

11. Early Explorers

1. Jacques Cartier
2. John Cabot
3. Samuel de Champlain
4. Jacques Cartier
5. John Cabot
6. Samuel de Champlain

12. Early Canadian History

1. The Vikings
2. L'Anse aux Meadows
3. The French and the Iroquois
4. The beaver
5. The Hudson's Bay Company
6. The fur-trade workers who travelled by canoe
7. The Battle of the Plains of Abraham
8. The British defeated the French

13. The Battle of the Plains of Abraham

1. T
2. F
3. T
4. T
5. T
6. F
7. F
8. T

14.After the Battle of the Plains of Abraham

1.Province of Quebec
2.habitants and Canadiens
3.Roman Catholic
4.1774
5.freedom
6.Quebec Act

15.United Empire Loyalists

1.1776
2.More than 40,000
3.To the Crown of England
4.Joseph Brant
5.Dutch, British, German, Scandinavian, and Aboriginal
6.Anglican, Baptist, Presbyterian, Methodist, Jewish, Catholic and Quaker religions
7. 3,000

16. Slavery in British North America

1.Lieutenant-Colonel John Graves Simcoe
2.Lieutenant-Colonel John Graves Simcoe
3.Toronto
4.1833
5.Mary Ann Shadd Cary
6.It was about anti-slavery, black immigration to Canada and about other moral and ethical principles
7.Escaped slaves from the United States.
8.It was a Christian network that helped smuggle black slaves into Canada.

17. The War of 1812 – Part 1

1. Chief Tecumseh
2. Major-General Sir Isaac Brock
3. Lietenant-Colonel Charles de Salaberry
4. Major-General Robert Ross
5. Laura Secord
6. Lieutenant James FitzGibbon

18. The War of 1812 – Part 2

1. The **United States of America** launched an invasion of the United States of America in 1812. T/**F**
2. British soldiers, Canadian volunteers and First Nations all worked together to defend Canada. **T**/F
3. Sir Isaac Brock was killed **at Queenston Heights**. T/**F**
4. Chief Tecumseh was a **Shawnee** leader. T/F
5. In 1813, Americans burned down parts of York (Toronto). **T**/F
6. Laura Secord warned the British of an American attack by **walking** for 30 km. T/**F**
7. The British **won** the Battle of Beaver Dams. T/**F**
8. By 1814 the Americans had lost the war. **T**/F

19. Before Confederation

1. Outside of Montreal and Toronto
2. Lord Durham
3. Lord Durham suggested that Upper Canada and Lower Canada be combined into one province, and that the new province should be given *responsible government*
4. 1840
5. 1847-48
6. Sir Louis-Hippolyte La Fontaine
7. Sir Leonard Tilley

20. Confederation – Part 1

1. 1867
2. Ontario
3. Sir George-Ettiene Cartier
4. Canada Day
5. The Dominion of Canada
6. Sir John A. Macdonald
7. Dominion Day
8. Legislature

21. Confederation – Part 2

1. 1867
2. July 1st, 1867
3. Ontario, Quebec, Nova Scotia and New Brunswick
4. Newfoundland and Labrador
5. Nunavut
6. Dominion Day
7. Sir John A Macdonald
8. Scotland
9. The ten-dollar bill
10. January 11

22.Confederation – Part 3

Province	Year
1.Ontario	**1867**
2.Prince Edward Island	**1873**
3.**British Columbia**	1871
4.**Nova Scotia**	1867
5.Alberta	**1905**
6.Quebec	**1867**
7.**Manitoba**	1870
8.**Saskatchewan**	1905
9.Newfoundland and Labrador	**1949**
10.New Brunswick	**1867**

Territory	Year
1.Norwest Territories	**1870**
2.Yukon	**1898**
3.**Nunavut**	1999

23.Louis Riel

1.Fort Garry
2.Métis
3.The United States of America
4.He was executed for treason
5.Gabriel Dumont
6.The North West Mounted Police (NWMP)
7.A mounted policeman and frontier hero.
8.The Royal Canadian Mounted Police (RCMP)

24. The Canadian Pacific Railway

1.1885
2.Lord Strathcona
3.unity
4.railway
5.Britsh Columbia
6.Sir Wilfrid Laurier
7.Ukranians
8.Head Tax

25.Women of Canada – Part 1

1.Manitoba
2.The right to vote
3.Dr.Emily Stowe
4.Sir Robert Borden
5.1918
6.Agnes Macphail
7.1940
8.Nurses who served in the Royal Canadian Army Medical Corps

26. Women of Canada – Part 2

1.Agnes Macphail
2.Therese Casgrain
3.Dr.Emily Stowe
4.The Bluebirds
5.Dr.Emily Stowe

27. The First World War – Part 1

1.1914
2.November 11, 1918
3.600,000
4.60,000
5.Sir Arthur Currie
6.Vimy Ridge
7.The Battle of Amiens

28. The First World War – Part 2

1. 600,000
2. 10,000
3. 11,1918
4. 60,000
5. 8,000
6. 1914
7. 9

29. Remembrance Day

1.November 11th
2.Lieutenant-Colonel John McCrae
3.He was a Canadian medical officer
4.A poppy
5.Observe a moment of silence
6.1915
7.*In Flanders fields the poppies blow,*
   Between the crosses, row on row,

30. The Second World War

1.1939
2.Over one million
3.The Royal Canadian Air Force
4.For mistreating and relocating Japanese-Canadians during the Second World War
5.D-Day
6. 15,000
7.May 8,1945
8.44,000

31. Post-War Canada

1.Oil was discovered in **Alberta** in 1947. T/**F**
2.Unemployment insurance was introduced in **1940**. T/**F**
3.Five hundred Canadians died during the Korean War (1950-53). **T**/F
4.The Official Languages Act of 1969 gave both English and French equal status in the government of Canada. **T**/F
5.The Canadian Constitution was amended in 1982. **T**/F
6.In **1970** Canada helped found La Francophonie. T/**F**
7.Japanese Canadians received the right to vote in **1948**. T/**F**
8.Aborginal people received the right to vote in 1960. **T**/F

32. Arts in Canada

Writers:
- **Rohinton Mistry**
- **Michael Odaatje**

Visual Artists:
- **Kenojuak Ashevak**
- **Emily Carr**

Filmmakers:
- **Atom Egoyan**
- **Denys Arcand**

Musicians:
- **Ernest Macmillan**
- **Healey Willan**

33. Sports in Canada

1. James Naismith
2. Lacrosse
3. Hockey
4. Terry Fox
5. Wayne Gretzky
6. Rick Hansen
7. Donovan Bailey
8. Paul Henderson

34. Inventions and Discoveries – Part 1

1. - e)
2. - g)
3. - a)
4. – h)
5. – b)
6. – c)
7. – d)
8. – f)

35. Inventions and Discoveries – Part 2

1. Sir Frederick Banting and Charles Best
2. Dr. John A. Hopps
3. Matthew Evans and Henry Woodward
4. Alexendar Graham Bell
5. Sir Sanford Fleming
6. Reginald Fessenden
7. Mike Lazaridis and Jim Balsillie
8. Joseph-Armand Bombardier

36. Canadian Government – Part 1

1. What are three important facts about Canada's system of government?
   - **It is a federal state**
   - **It is a parliamentary democracy**
   - **It is a constitutional monarchy**
2. What are the three parts of Parliament?
   - **The Sovereign (Queen or King)**
   - **The House of Commons**
   - **The Senate**
3. What are the three branches of the Canadian Government?
   - **The Executive Branch**
   - **The Legislative Branch**
   - **The Judicial Branch**

37. Canadian Government – Part 2

1. Defence, foreign policy, currency, trade, etc.
2. The House of Commons
3. The Prime Minister
4. Senators
5. A bill is a draft copy of a proposed law
6. Royal Assent
7. The Sovereign (King or Queen of England)
8. The Prime Minister

38. Canadian Government – Part 3

1. Governor General
2. Senator
3. Prime Minister
4. Member of Parliament
5. Lieutenant Governor
6. Premier
7 Sovereign
8. Commissioner

39. Federal Elections in Canada – Part 1

1. On the third Monday of October every four years
2. 338
3. A Member of Parliament
4. Who can vote in elections? List three criteria.

   - Canadian Citizen
   - 18 or older
   - On the voters' list

5. A Majority Government
6. A Minority Government

40. Federal Elections – Part 2

1. The Prime Minister
2. A Cabinet Minister is in charge of a federal department
3. The Official Opposition (or Her Majesty's Loyal Opposition)

41. Federal Government – Questions

Use an Internet search engine to find out who your political representatives are.

42. Municipal Government

1. Mayor
4. by-laws
5. What are three responsibilities of a municipal government?

- Snow removal
- recycling
- policing
- firefighting
- transportation

43. Provincial Government

5. What are three responsibilities of a provincial government?

- Education
- Health care
- Highways

44. Justice in Canada

1. In Canada, you are **innocent** until proven **guilty**. T/**F**

2. In Canada, the law applies to everyone. **T**/F

3. The Supreme Court of Canada is Canada's highest court. **T**/F

4. The RCMP is Canada's federal police force. **T**/F

5. Ontario and **Quebec** have their own provincial police force. T/**F**

6. The RCMP serves as the provincial police force in all provinces other than **Ontario and Quebec**. T/**F**

45. The Symbols of Canada – Part 1

1. – f)
2. – c)
3. – a)
4. – g)
5. – d)
6. – e)
7. – h)
8. – b)

46. The Symbols of Canada – Part 2

1. 400 years
2. 1965
3. Lacrosse
4. It was destroyed by a fire
5. 1927
6. *A mari usque ad mare* (from sea to sea)
7. 1948
8. The Maple Leaf

47. The Crown in Canada

1. O Canada
2. God Save the Queen (or King)
3. The Union Jack
4. 1965
5. Queen Victoria
6. The Governor General

48. The Victoria Cross

1. Ninety-six
2. Lieutenant Alexander Roberts Dunn
3. Billy Bishop
4. Able Seaman William Hall
5. Lieutenant Robert Hampton Gray
6. Corporal Filip Konowal
7. The Second World War

49. The Canadian Economy

1. Canada, Mexico and the United States of America
2. 1988
3. What are Canada's three main types of industries?

   - Service
   - Manufacturing
   - Natural Resources

4. Service
5. Natural Resources
6. Manufacturing
7. The United States of America
8. Over seventy-five percent

50. Canadian Geography – Questions

1. The Atlantic, Pacific and Arctic Oceans
2. Ottawa
3. 1857
4. Ten provinces and three territories
5. Over thirty-five million
6. Five
7. What are the five regions of Canada?

- The Atlantic Provinces
- Central Canada
- The Prairie Provinces
- The West Coast
- The Northern Territories

51. The Regions of Canada – Part 1

1. The Atlantic Provinces
   - Newfound and Labrador
   - Nova Scotia
   - New Brunswick
   - Prince Edward Island

2. Central Canada
   - Quebec
   - Ontario

3. The Prairie Provinces
   - Manitoba
   - Saskatchewan
   - Alberta

4. The West Coast
   - British Columbia

5. The Northern Territories
   - Nunavut
   - Northwest Territories
   - Yukon Territory

52. Regions of Canada – Part 2

1. The Northern Territories
2. Central Canada
3. The Atlantic Provinces
4. The Prairie Provinces
5. The West Coast
6. The Northern Territories
7. Central Canada
8. The Northern Territories

53. The Regions of Canada – Part 3

Region	Provinces or Territories
• The West Coast	• **British Columbia**
• **The Prairie Provinces**	• Alberta • **Manitoba** • **Saskatchewan**
• Central Canada	• **Ontario** • **Quebec**
• **The Atlantic Provinces**	• Prince Edward Island • **Nova Scotia** • **New Brunswick** • Newfoundland and Labrador
• The Northern Territories	• **Nunavut** • **Northwest Territories** • **Yukon Territory**

54. The Canadian Provinces
1. Quebec
2. Nova Scotia
3. Newfoundland and Labrador
4. New Brunswick
5. British Columbia
6. Prince Edward Island
7. Nunavut
8. Alberta
9. Manitoba
10. Yukon
11. Ontario
12. Saskatchewan
13. Northwest Territories

55. The Provincial and Territorial Capitals

Province	Capital
British Columbia	**Victoria**
Saskatchewan	Regina
New Brunswick	Fredericton
Alberta	**Edmonton**
Prince Edward Island	**Charlottetown**
Quebec	Quebec City
Ontario	**Toronto**
Manitoba	**Winnipeg**
Nova Scotia	Halifax
Newfoundland and Labrador	St.John's

Territory	Capital
Yukon	**Whitehorse**
Nunavut	Iqaluit
Northwest Territories	**Yellowknife**

56. The Capital Cities

1.British Columbia
2.New Brunswick
3.Saskatchewan
4.Nova Scotia
5.Ontario
6.Nunavut
7.Prince Edward Island
8.Yukon Territory
9.Newfoundland and Labrador
10.Alberta
11.Quebec
12.Northwest Territories
13.Manitoba

57. Canadian Provinces and Territories

1.**Newbrunswick** is the only officially bilingual province.
2.The capital of British Columbia is **Victoria.**
3.The Mackenzie River is located in **Northwest Territories**.
4.**Alberta** is home to Banff National Park.
5.**Halifax** is the largest port on the east coast of Canada.
6.**Montreal** is Canada's second largest city.
7.**British Columbia** is known for the fruit and wine industries of the Okanagan Valley.
8.**Prince Edward Island** is the birthplace of Confederation.

58. Review Questions – Part 1

1.What are three important aspects about Canada's system of government?
- **It is a federal state**
- **It is a parliamentary democracy**
- **It is a constitutional monarchy**

2.What are the three levels of government in Canada?
- **Federal**
- **Provincial/Territorial**
- **Municipal**

3.What are the three branches of government in Canada?
- **Executive**
- **Legislative**
- **Judicial**

4.What are the three parts of Parliament?
- **The Sovereign (King or Queen)**
- **The House of Commons**
- **The Senate**

59. Review Questions – Part 2

1.Who are the three founding peoples of Canada?
- **The Aboriginal**
- **The British**
- **The French**

2.What are the three distinct Aboriginal peoples of Canada?
- **First Nations**
- **Métis**
- **Inuit**

3.The Prime Minister
4.The Sovereign (King or Queen)
5.New Brunswick

60.Review Questions – Political Review

Use an Internet search engine to find out who your political representatives are.

My Notes

My Notes

My Notes

My Notes

My Notes

My Notes

My Notes

My Notes

Manufactured by Amazon.ca
Bolton, ON